LIFE on the ICE

SUSAN E. GOODMAN

LIFE
on the ICE

with photographs by
MICHAEL J. DOOLITTLE

M Millbrook Press • Minneapolis

To the men and women of the New York Air National Guard 109th Airlift Wing and the National Science Foundation. They help make polar discoveries possible — and gave us the adventure of a lifetime.

Millbrook Press
A division of Lerner Publishing Group
241 First Avenue North
Minneapolis, Minnesota 55401 U.S.A.
Website address: www.lernerbooks.com

Library of Congress Cataloging-in-Publication Data

Goodman, Susan E., 1952–
    Life on the ice / by Susan E. Goodman ; photographs by
Michael J. Doolittle.
       p.   cm.
    ISBN-13: 978–0–7613–2775–2 (lib. bdg. : alk. paper)
    ISBN-10: 0–7613–2775–4 (lib. bdg. : alk. paper)
    1. Polar regions—Description and travel—Juvenile literature.
I. Doolittle, Michael J., ill. II. Title.
G587.G66 2006
910'.911—dc22   2005006141

Manufactured in the United States of America
1 2 3 4 5 6 – JR – 11 10 09 08 07 06

Acknowledgments

We'd like to thank Major Robert Bullock of the 109th and Jim Fuchs, formerly captain in the U.S. Air Force, for bringing us aboard and making sure this project went smoothly. Thanks to all the men and women of the 109th for their support, especially Flight Engineer Maurice Huard who answered so many of our questions. Kaj-Gunnar Sievert provided an international perspective and Dena Headlee at the National Science Foundation helped us track down and confirm many of our facts. At Millbrook, thanks to designer Robin Hoffmann for her exciting layout and editor Jean Reynolds for all her enthusiasm.

Photo Acknowledgments

Additional photographs are reproduced with permission from: Wayne Papps, ©Australian Antarctic Division, Commonwealth of Australia, front cover main; **National Oceanic and Atmospheric Administration Central Library Photo Collection:** (Michael Van Woert, NOAA NESDIS, ORA) front cover people, (Commander John Bortniak) back cover, p. 11, (Michael Van Woert) pp. 2, 8 top, 9, (NOAA Corps Collection) p. 25 top, (Lieutenant Philip Hall) p. 30 top left, (Budd Christman) p. 30 right; **NASA,** p. 5; **© Bryan & Cherry Alexander,** p. 6; **National Science Foundation:** (Josh Landis) p. 8 bottom, (Jeffrey Kietzmann) p. 10, (Mark Buckley) p. 14, (Melanie Conner) pp. 19 bottom left, 21 left, (Jonathan Berry) p. 19 right, (Mark Sabbatini) p. 24, (Michael Poole) p. 25 bottom, (Lynn Teo Simarski) p. 29, (Aaron Spitzer), p. 31; **United States Air Force, Photo by 109th Airlift Wing Multimedia Center,** pp. 16, 22 both, 23 both, 27; **Mark Twickler, University of New Hampshire,** p. 17 right; **Antarctic Search for Meteorites Program:** p. 18 left, (Jamie Pierce) p. 18 right; **R. Lowenstein/Center for Astrophysical Research in Antarctica,** p. 19 top left; **Steven C. Amstrup,** p. 30 bottom left.

The top and the
bottom of our planet
are covered with ice.

The top, the Arctic, is home to the North Pole.
It can be so cold that a cup of hot water, thrown in
the air, will explode into a cloud of ice particles.

THE NORTH POLE IS LOCATED IN THE MIDDLE OF THE ARCTIC OCEAN AND IS USUALLY COVERED BY ICE.

The South Pole is at the bottom of our planet on the continent of Antarctica. This region is even colder than the Arctic, sometimes plunging to −125°F (−52°C). In winter, parts of the oceans surrounding Antarctica freeze over, doubling its size.

Antarctica is the coldest, driest, windiest place on Earth. It is so isolated that no human had even seen this continent until two hundred years ago.

THE ICE COVERING ANTARCTICA
CONTAINS ABOUT 70 PERCENT OF
THE WORLD'S FRESHWATER.

ICEBERGS CAN BE AS SMALL AS
A PIANO OR LARGER THAN A
SMALL COUNTRY.

Places this cold, this extreme, are hard to imagine.

In fall the sun sets and doesn't rise again for the entire winter. Months later, it shines twenty-four hours a day—all summer long.

Even though they are covered by ice, these regions are deserts—dry like the Sahara. Very little snow falls in either place. But when it does, it rarely melts. Over time, the snow becomes ice—in some places, almost three miles (5 km) thick.

This ice is slowly moving, inching from the middle of the Arctic and Antarctica to their coasts. By the time pieces break off into the ocean and become icebergs, the ice is 100,000 years old.

People fly thousands of miles to reach the Poles. And when the winds kick up and blow the snow around, it's hard to know where the sky ends and the land begins. Pilots say that it's like flying inside a Ping-Pong ball.

Many of the instruments normally used to guide planes won't work there. In fact, navigators flying to the Poles are the only ones left in the U.S. Air Force who still help map their route with the stars. This is some of the hardest flying there is.

MOST ANTARCTIC "BLIZZARDS" OCCUR
WHEN SNOW ON THE GROUND IS WHIPPED
AROUND BY THE STRONGEST WINDS ON
EARTH. THE SKY OVERHEAD IS BLUE, WHILE
PEOPLE ON LAND CANNOT SEE THEIR
HANDS IN FRONT OF THEM.

Planes do not land in these wintry worlds by rolling down
concrete runways. They use skis instead. And they slide like
giant sleds until they stop.

Gliding along, the skis get so hot that they melt the snow
they're resting on. Pilots must pull them up when the planes
stop. Otherwise, the wet snow would refreeze on the skis and
the planes would be stuck to the ground.

WHEN PILOTS LAND AT THE SOUTH
POLE, THEY KEEP THEIR ENGINES
RUNNING. IT'S SO COLD THAT THEY
MIGHT NOT START UP AGAIN.

Sounds like an adventure story, doesn't it? It *is* an adventure story—one with science. Scientists are today's explorers, braving the wilderness to learn more about our world.

The snow near the North Pole, for example, hasn't melted since the last ice age. Over 100,000 years of it has been pressed into an ice sheet almost 2 miles (3.2 km) thick. But each layer looks separate, like the rings of a tree.

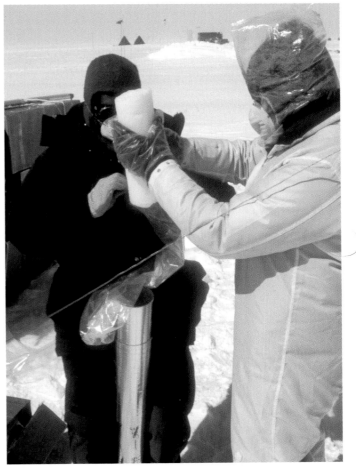

Some scientists use this snow to measure air pollution. Others are drilling through this ice to pull out history. Each sample they bring up tells a story about the time when it was formed. Scientists have found volcanic ash from Italy's Mount Vesuvius, for instance, and pollution from ancient Roman times.

Scientists began this experiment to learn more about how ice ages begin and end. Before, they thought our climate needed thousands of years to change. Now they know it can happen much, much faster.

WHEN THIS ICE MELTS, IT CRACKLES AND FIZZES AS BUBBLES RELEASE AIR THAT HAS BEEN TRAPPED INSIDE FOR UP TO 100,000 YEARS.

At the South Pole some scientists search for meteorites, rocks from outer space. Meteorites are no more likely to fall there than anywhere else on Earth. But, as one scientist explains, if you want to find something dark, it's easier to look on a big white sheet. His team has given thousands of meteorites to our space agency, the National Aeronautics and Space Administration (NASA) for study.

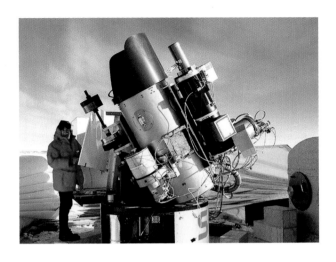

The Antarctic sky is a perfect window to the stars, the best on this planet. It is very clear because it's so cold and dry—and has a night that is six months long. Some scientists use telescopes to study the age of the universe. Others fly balloons to measure rays coming in from outer space.

IN WINTER THE ANTARCTIC SKY IS PAINTED WITH AURORAS, BEAUTIFUL LIGHTS THAT SHIMMER WHEN PARTICLES FROM SPACE MEET UP WITH THE EARTH'S ATMOSPHERE.

At the Poles people wear many layers of clothing to keep warmth in and wind out. They wear big boots and overalls called fat-boy pants. Their mittens have furry backs to wipe their noses and warm their ears.

They also wear goggles. Without them, their eyes would get sunburned and temporarily blinded by the strong light bouncing off the snow.

NO WEARING RINGS,
EARRINGS, OR SUNGLASSES
WITH METAL FRAMES IN THE
EXTREME COLD. METAL GETS SO
COLD THAT IT WILL FREEZE ANY
SKIN THAT IT TOUCHES.

People who work at the Poles must learn how to survive being stuck outdoors. On an unexpected "camping trip," they first build a quick shelter to get out of the wind. Then they build a better one and pack in close to one another, using body heat to stay warm.

Building shelters—doing any work—is much harder in extreme cold. Mittens are very bulky, but it's unsafe to go bare-handed for long. Getting too cold is dangerous, but so is getting overheated. Sweat can freeze into a layer of ice next to your body.

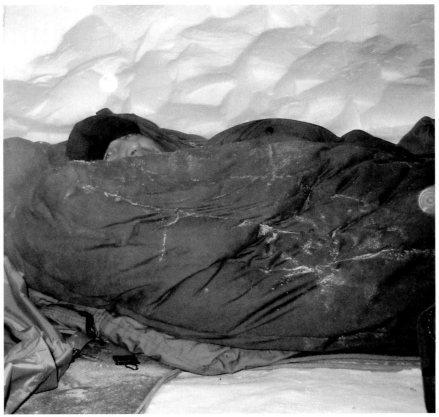

UNLIKE MOST REFRIGERATORS, THE ONE CONTAINING FRUIT AND VEGETABLES AT THE SOUTH POLE IS HEATED.

In summer many people live at the science stations in the Arctic and Antarctica. They have a gym and videos and spend their spare time skiing on the icy runways. But mostly they work hard, getting as much done as possible while the weather is warm enough for planes to fly in and out.

A few of them stay all winter long. Scientists say that summer's constant daylight tricks your body into wanting to keep going without rest. But in winter's endless darkness, you feel tired much of the time. One scientist even studies the people who winter-over at the South Pole. He wants to know what kind of person works well in such a small, isolated group. Someday his findings may help pick the people to live in a colony on Mars.

In spring in Antarctica, the temperature finally climbs up to −50°F (−10°C) and it's warm enough for planes to fly in again. The scientists are eager to get on board and return to the colors and smells of the "green world."

Once they buckle up, there is one last frosty problem to solve. The airplane must go 100 miles (160 km) per hour to take off, no easy task when sliding over ice. Sometimes pilots must taxi 2 miles (3 km) to reach that speed. And sometimes they need extra help. Then they turn to the eight rockets attached to their plane.

A flick of the switch, a burst of flames and speed, and . . .

. . . they are on their way home.

The Planes

It takes professional pilots three years to learn to fly the LC–130, the largest airplane on skis. The New York Air National Guard 109th Airlift Wing, part of the United States Air Force, flies these "ski-birds" to the Arctic and Antarctica. They help the National Science Foundation get scientists and supplies to the most remote places on Earth.

When they fly, each soldier takes an emergency bag with extreme cold-weather clothing. They also load the plane with warm sleeping bags, sleds, and enough food and water for a week. They never know when a storm will force them to the ground. They even bring snow shovels in case they must dig out their plane.

Despite the danger, most members of the 109th think they have the best mission in the world. They go places that few other people have ever been. They see icebergs and whales, polar bears and penguins. "Best of all," said one pilot, "we're helping science."

The Polar Regions

The Arctic and Antarctica are almost the same size. But the Arctic is an ice-covered sea surrounded by three continents. Antarctica is a continent, surrounded by oceans.

The earth actually has two North Poles—and two South Poles too. The geographic North Pole is the very top of our planet. It lies in the middle of the Arctic Ocean. The magnetic North Pole is the *N* that compasses point to. The exact location of that pole changes all the time. The geographic South Pole is on Antarctica, and the magnetic one is in the Antarctic Ocean.

Why are these regions so cold? The Earth is slightly tilted as it circles around the sun. This tilt, plus the curve of the planet, makes the sunlight shining on the Arctic and Antarctica spread over a wider area. A thick layer of air soaks up a lot of the heat before it hits the ground. Then the snow is like a mirror that reflects much of the sun's energy. And that is what happens in the summer, when there *is* sunshine! In winter the tilt of the earth keeps the sun from shining on these regions for months!

The Arctic is home to polar bears, walrus and seals, white whales called belugas, and black killer whales called orcas. Antarctica is so cold that no big animals actually live there. But seals and penguins spend time on its coast and feed from the surrounding seas.

Polar Science

At both poles scientists are seeking the answers to many questions. In the Arctic, for example, they are measuring temperatures, wind speeds, and snowfalls. These facts will help them decide if our weather is truly getting warmer worldwide Some scientists watch the health of polar bears. Others have put a tracking device on a ringed seal. Using a radio, they are learning where these animals go during their yearly migrations

Still other scientists patrol the Arctic Ocean on huge ships. They have discovered a dozen volcanoes rising from the ocean floor, firing hot lava into the freezing waters.

Scientists also travel the continent of Antarctica, studying everything from the ice to the fossils underneath that show this land had lush, green forests 270 million years ago.

They are even studying native plants and animals of today. On the coast, for example, some scientists dive below the ice sheet to study penguins. In fact, they've learned that penguins are amazing divers themselves, plunging one-third of a mile (half a kilometer) into the icy sea during one dive.

Other scientists are going fishing. They have discovered that local fish have a kind of antifreeze in their blood that keeps them from freezing solid in the ocean's 28°F (2°C) water. These chemicals "find" tiny ice crystals in the fish's body and don't let them grow any bigger.

Although seven countries have claimed territory there, no country owns Antarctica. It has been set aside as a land devoted to peace and science.

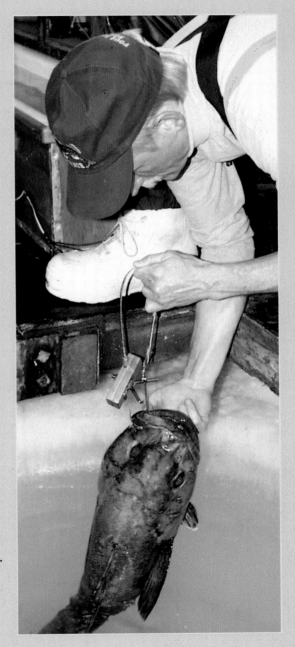

Bibliography

Alexander, Bryan and Cherry. *Journey into the Arctic*. New York: Oxford University Press, 2003.

Curlee, Lynn. *Into the Ice: The Story of Arctic Exploration*. Boston: Houghton Mifflin Company, 1998.

Dewey, Jennifer Owings. *Antarctic Journal: Four Months at the Bottom of the World*. New York: HarperCollins Publishers, 2001.

Johnson, Rebecca L. *Braving the Frozen Frontier: Women Working in Antarctica*. Minneapolis: Lerner Publications Company, 1997.

Johnson, Rebecca L. *Science on the Ice: An Antarctic Journal*. Minneapolis: Lerner Publications Company, 1995.

Lambert, David. *Polar Regions*. Morristown, NJ: Silver Burdett Press, 1988.

Pringle, Laurence. *Antarctica: The Last Unspoiled Continent*. New York: Simon and Schuster Books for Young Readers, 1992.

Index

About the Author and Photographer

To research their books, Susan E. Goodman and Michael J. Doolittle have climbed up to the top of a New York skyscraper and traveled down the Amazon River. This time they took off from a military base in New York State and landed in the Arctic Circle. While on this adventure, they ate musk ox, kept pens and cameras inside jackets so they'd be warm enough to work, and cursed the daylight that kept them awake at 3 o'clock in the morning. They were glad they didn't need to build an emergency igloo out on the ice; they liked experiencing the sense of dangerous adventure—but without the danger part. Visit Susan at www.susangoodmanbooks.com.